LETTERS TO THE HINTERLAND

Roy McFadden

The Dedalus Press
46 Seabury, Sydney Parade Avenue, Sandymount, Dublin 4

ISBN 0 948268 15 8 (paper)
ISBN 0 948268 14 X (bound)
2/11/89

The Dedalus Press acknowledges the financial assistance of the Arts
Council of Northern Ireland in the publication of this book.

Typesetting & make-up: Vermilion
Cover design: Brendan Foreman

Contents

2 SEPTEMBER 1939

At ease, basking in talk, as if
Respectful distances deferred,
Giving him time, the dandelion light
Already sentimental on the wall,
He stands forever graced by that afternoon:
Which I, looking for something else,
Thoughtlessly stumble on, as if
All the dead-and-gone had still to arrive
With ribbons and flowers, or wreaths under
    their arms.

34 TITE STREET

Houses, whose plaques commemorate
Poet, musician, painter, architect,
Tracked down and photographed
By zealous tourist, jealous devotee,
Continue, unimpressed,
Preoccupied with the domestic round.

Take, for example, 34
Tite Street, in Chelsea; whited sepulchre
In Oscar's heyday, when,
Groomed, self-composed, he lingered on the steps
Adjusting his lapels,
Verse on his lips and bad boys on his mind;

And when, after they'd cornered him,
Rightminded and rampaging citizens
Sacked the exotic rooms
And plundered relics from the sacrifice
Of his magnificence,
While, further off, whores roistered in the street;

And when, abandoned, it shrank back
Into the terrace's conformity,
Toeing the thin red line,
From camouflage to commonplace, inside
The floors and stairs retained
Their spring for each new decade at the door.

Today, pausing to contemplate
The banished ogre's fairy palace, you
Stumble upon respect
For underrated hereditaments,
That, imperturbably,
Clean up the droppings after each demise.

STYLE

Bedside companion —
The lady nobly dying,
Murmuring I will see you there —
Soignée, articulate, you dignified
Goodbye for me as well:
Whatever distances you undertake,
May you arrive in style.

A friend had taken my arm
To indicate you in the street,
Pronounce with passionate concern:
Young poets, lacking confidence and style,
Require an older, educated love,
Thirty-or-so; intelligent: and, o,
Sophisticated, exquisitely heeled.

VICTORIES

Some still remember how
Caraciola in
The white Mercedes stormed
Majestically to victory through the rain;
And, later, Nuvolari, tanned
Under the goggles, lifted an elegant glove
Dappled with dust to greet the chequered cheers.

The district councillor,
Safe in the family car,
Switched the ignition on
And settled down to nurse the engine's cough.
Goodbye, they called into the dark.
All hell broke loose, they cried; and, later, he
Was spelt out from the fragments in the park.

LOS DESPARECIDOS

Forcing the frames, the windows sang.
Seconds before the gable crashed,
Gulls, turning tail, dived back to sea,
The nervous suburbs barked;
And, brokenbacked, walls staggered, hand on heart,
After defecting stairs.

Now you, who strummed on railings or
Sheltered in doorways, climbed the stairs,
May hoist a black flag overhead
For vanished citizens;
And fasten, if you like, on your lapel
A black contorted key.

OLD MR KERSHAW

Affronted and afraid,
The tentative greeting crumpled, pocketed;
    Perhaps alerted too
Against intrusion on a solitude
    That tended the torn stare
And turned his hearing to oracular shells,
I recognised that he was not all there.

    Slow to identify
The trudging stranger with the family friend,
    Respected, amiable;
Eyes following defecting distances,
    With the myopic gaze
Over his glasses as my father talked —
I sidled from his new, prophetic face:

    Too young and ignorant
To apprehend inside the guttering coat,
    The flaring scarecrow sleeves,
His huge intolerance of civilities
    Distracting him like flies
From fierce perusal of the palimpsest
For words to stem the panic in his eyes.

THE COLONEL

When I was a child he lived on up the hill.
His grass and garden paths were derelict.
Though almost dashing, he lacked elegance.
On milder days he sported on his arm
A wife who looked much older, wickeder.
And, though they had a vestibule,
They kept the front door shut against the street.
Remarkably, they'd neither child nor dog.
He seemed far too important for hallo.
His groomed moustache suggested the Great War.

When I was ten we moved across the town.
He stayed, with childhood, in the hinterland,
A character inside a nursery tale,
A giant, good or bad, secure within
A legendary ever-ever land.
So, later, when I came upon a grey
Clerk at a counter, clipping documents,
It was his alter ego that assumed
The guise of unassuming citizen.
Back home, the implacable hero swung his cane.

All through the war he harried editors
With forecasts of disaster. Never since
Has *Northern Whig* or *Belfast News Letter*
Been so oracular without his name
Beneath the hardboiled *Yours etcetera.*
He argued for relentless war
From Stalingrad to Ballyhackamore;
Included every German cat and dog
In massive extirpation. *The poor things,*
My mother said, in ridicule and rage.

14

Now, after half a lifetime, I observe
Him in the town, like an old masher with
His tilted hat, his angled walking-stick,
The shoes alas no longer glittering,
The strict moustache still bristling for salute:
Glancing at shops and offices
As if expecting to be summoned in
To overhaul the system, improvise
A firing squad to line up in the yard
And execute the latest dissidents.

Young cashiers at the counter in the bank
Think he's an officer (retired). *Colonel,*
The one with tinted spectacles declares;
He cashes monthly cheques made out like that.
We peer inquiringly to where he's furled
But watchful by the rubber-plant,
Plotting new strategies perhaps, or still
Exterminating Germans; or perhaps —
Allow for wounds behind the uniform —
Just being old, and lonely, and afraid.

THE HOUSE

The house was built in a dry summer
On a virgin hillside of grass
Under a motionless sky in bee-dazed air.
The girl smoothed mirrored hair to meet her love.

Autumn dulled to bronze
The summer's brasses, but
The soil remembered and stirred,
And in the captive garden
Burgeoning then she knelt down to embrace
A leaf's complicity.
And the alice-blue dress was stained
With the grass of that last summer.

Today, after thirty years
Of burnt-out summers, I viewed,
Aloof on a faded floor,
A woman dead; the door strangely ajar,
The wireless lisping, and the red
Metal lips of the fire implacably dumb:
And the hillside levelled and drained
To meet the marching suburbs of the town —
As though I had never breathed, in the dazed air
Over the rush-harsh grass,
The word of a young girl's name, the sky
Becalmed in her eyes and the sun putting gold in her
        hair.

THE DEN

She called it The Den; the name
Persisting from girlhood,, when passion and languors
    vied
In albums and diaries.
In the garden, the nesting-boxes had names for the
    birds.

The outlook anthologised
Decades of borders, rockeries, arbours and
(Not wildly incongruous)
Field-flowers permitted to roam, indulged like a child.

In her hat with the veil, and her hands
Majestic with lace or chaste in diaphonous gloves,
She established herself in a world
Where china and chat discouraged the cry from the
    heart.

But, for unbelievers, The Den
With the crack in the ceiling and damp like a hand on
    the wall,
And yesterday's flowers in the vase,
Had the look of a room abandoned by children and
    love;

Where, remote from the window, with age
Uncovered in neck and hands, she discarded her day's
Coiffured appearances, and
Exhumed the cry in her heart, and said o my love

Let them scatter my death in the wind;
For the house will defect, and neglect to reflect or recall
The Den and its denizen, when
They have covered the crack and coped with the hand
    on the wall.

FIRST BLOOD

When you and Kernaghan
Fought in the cellars, it began
With formal insults, ritualistically.
Exchanges petered out, and counsellors
Demanded violence;
Squeezed back and shuffled to a square,
And roared on gestures hurled
Over the arms and shoulders like balloons.
It was a game:
A bout of shadow-boxing; pantomine.

But once when Kernaghan
Provoked Maginess where he stood
Foresquare against the latrine's steaming wall,
There was no pussy-footing argument,
Naming of seconds, or
A kiss-my-hand and pas-de-deux;
But unabashed mayhem:
Tapped claret ugly outside schoolboy slang.
And we recoiled,
Not yet conditioned to the acts of war.

FIRE BOMB

McKelvey watched from his baulked car
The corrugating fire consume
And lick the building clean; but for
The casual citizen hurrying home
The gathering smoke, he said, might seem
Familiar weather.

Be careful not to generalise
In anger, he rebuked his thought,
And censure nihilists en masse;
Distinguish between this and that
Obscenity, each tit for tat:
Particularise.

He'd never loved his native town;
But now with buildings torn apart,
His generation's bridges blown,
New generations forced apart,
He could not quench his smouldering heart
With cold disdain.

SIDE WARD

The trouble is we never believe it,
That the moment of truth, in a manner of speaking —
Reserving of course our own improbable deaths —
Is always now. But we never see it,
Until the moment is past, and the scent's gone cold;
And then, as often as not, the retrospection's
A new creation nurturing itself.

You could specify each *then*; advancing
Examples of *you* and *yours*, the *you*
Being notionally constant, but the *yours*
Shifting from childhood to age, and suddenly strange.
And the mood, on reflection, is not
Nostalgia; it is regret: for the children who run
Out into the garden to play, and vanish for ever.

So sit in your shining cell, deferring
To hospital sounds and the traffic of trolleys,
To patients' petulance, the patter of staff,
The demented lady demanding her longlost home:
In a whitefaced room unkindled by live light,
Outfacing the moment now, the fact of your being
Assigned to a faceless man with a knife in his hand.

SHOP SOIL

Suspiration of leaves
Snatched from submissive fields
Assails your frontiers, infiltrates
Your settled suburbs; and, a child,
You stand for hymns at harvest festivals.

Headstrong chrysanthemums,
Unbending merchandise,
You say address a hinterland
Where each aborted journey waits
For redirection by the traveller;

Where fugitives converge
From extirpated lives,
Survivors from the dark,
Trailing lame roots of memory
Back to the daydream of the marigold.

INTERPOLATION

One reading, Rilke, is that life elects
For breaking those who come too close to it.
Chosen, you knew how hard it is to thole
In silent abnegation. Nobody
Sends thunder skittling through the clouds or claps
A hand of darkness on the midday sun.
Nor can we say to anyone *Forgive*.
The house we built in springtime tumbles down,
And hindsight excavates the running sand.
Eurydice is buried in the dark
In bright midsummer mourned by petulant trees
Shrugging off sunshine. Think how Orpheus —
Then silent as the grave, when all he touched
(Advised beforehand) turned away from him
As something separate, intended, pledged
To other meanings — looked into their eyes
And saw in them his own disfigurement.
When he persisted, they dismembered him.

DOCTOR SERAFICO

1. The Muzot Event

Unwavering guardian of his solitude's
Establishment
In fortresses moated by distances,
He ruthlessly
Discountenanced ambitious canvassers,
New loves intent on rearranging him,
Old loves with querulous wounds.

And studied, cultivated silences;
And, stoically,
Put up with disappointment and despair;
Was sceptical
Of hearkening trees and hurrying steps in the rain:
For the Angels enter unheard, their luminous
Presence immediate.

Waiting, he sifted, sounded out his words;
And disciplined
Structures and rhythms, the obliging rhyme,
Bold metaphors —
(You must change your life) — for metamorphosis
To statures shrugging off the sculptor's hand,
The outgrown scaffolding.

But when they came at last, his separateness
Seethed into storm.
Whole days and nights he worked translating them,
Groaning aloud,
Until the agony and ecstasy
Expelled the unforgiving miracle,
And he broke from the cord.

Then he looked round, restored to furniture:
Assuredly
Heard thrushes singing in the startling rain,
And, from the town,
An arching shout buoyed up and lightly held
High in the air until it thinned and fell
Silent everywhere.

Adjusting vision back to surfaces,
To round and rind,
He groped for speech like coins or peppermints,
A clutch of keys:
And when he ventured out among the trees,
He marvelled that the untransmuted scene
Could still seem probable.

Then he wrote letters, propping up his hand.
— To the Princess:
At last, at last the blessed, blessed day.
— To Kippenberg:
I didn't know such storms could be survived.
Reprieved, he stroked the rough patrolling walls,
And fingered the moon's caress.

2. After Muzot
Depleted then;
Enormously bereft:
He signalled from the castle walls
Deliverance from his solitude;
And, when they sent for him,
Bowed to applause.

They fêted him
In salons, but their praise
Was for accomplishments before
He cried out to the Angels. Thus,
No one commended him
For altering Life.

Garrulous then —
Head upon shoulder, hands
Italicised, extravagant —
He seemingly apostrophised
Celestial auditors,
Seraphically.

Discountenanced,
They shrugged, and turned away;
While, fettered to his monologue,
Eyes mesmerised by distances,
He fretfully recalled
Incredible wings.

3. *Marthe*
Perhaps he followed her.
But far more likely it was she
Accosted him with casual impudence.
But, anyhow,
Their lives collided; he retrieved,
As you might say, her crumpled handkerchief.

Footloose at seventeen,
She bit on rinds while he
Suffered the sweetness for the core.
Fastidiously,
He waived her body for her mind,
Which opened up, he said, to his hard verse.

Street-singer Orpheus!
His letters to the dear Princess
Intrigued her, convalescent in the sun.
She marvelled how
A little girl, catching his sleeve,
Could coax his solitude to follow her.

After his style, he found
A *pied-à-terre* inside her heart.
He, who loved roses, bought her violets;
And suffered her,
On tiptoe at the gutter's edge,
To fasten her quick choice to his lapel.

4. *An Honourable Death*
Seeing his death
As life's associate,
A sleeping-partner or co-parcener,
Quiescent, reticent —
He pictured his dying as
The gradual dissolution of a room,
The slow recession of an afternoon
From books and furniture;
A congregation of friends,
Voices gloved in the dark,
Attending and participating in
A modest ceremony of goodbye.

How different then,
When, surging up in him
Perversely in their common residence
It tunnelled through his veins
To burst in sibilant sores
Whose incoherence lacked interpreters,
Whose mouths decried impervious presences,
Inert, inflexible wings.

But he persisted; still
Electing to command
The rhythm of his dying: to endure,
And honour his commitment to the end.

TELLING

You too, he said, have seen
Styles come and go, modes, fashions change.
The match's head
Flared into transient flame; contentedly
He nestled in companionable smoke.

The reddening core engaged,
He shook the smouldering splinter dead,
And said that all
Variety of manner is a sheath
That flight makes, or the rocked wake on the sea.

POETRY READING

I know you. Having climbed the stairs
Of elderly buildings through the years
To public meetings, rallies, conferences
For culture, justice, peace,
Here at the top I recognise
The same decrepitude:
Cracked ceilings, decadent walls and cupboard-smells,
And, underneath, mouse-furtive silences.

And contemplate resemblances
In tentative faces at the door,
Muted or caricatured in middle-age:
Life's nonparticipants,
Spinsters and tidy bachelors,
Obliging furniture
For long-dead skivvies' loveless attic-rooms,
Abandoned or forgotten by the town.

I know the poet too; or did,
When he was young and adamant,
And living called for more than livelihood.
But, grown professional,
Paid for the act, the one-night stand,
More than the verse commands,
He works the system of establishment,
Whose imprimatur is his business-card.

He finds marked pages in his book
For prefatory paraphrase.
They listen secretly, or elevate
To high grey windowlight
Aspiring or despairing eyes,

Drugged by the monotone,
The trudging traffic of his images,
A substitute for summer in the blood.

Closing, he makes an actor's bow,
One hand adjacent to the heart.
But hungry voices remonstrate, and he
Reads out another page,
An encore, if you like, for love,
Then smiles, and deprecates.
Chairs back and bark; and hasty hands applaud.
They line up for the plastic autograph.

He packs his bag, shrugs on his anorak,
And shuts up shop;
Then softly goes
Back to the safe street where he parked the car.

OIL PAINTING: THE MANSE AT RALOO

Late March perhaps was breaking
  Disdainfully into spring, unable
To nip in the bud the catching laughter of leaves;
  Or autumn itself had turned
  Its coat, defecting to hare-lipped horns
As winter blazed a trail for coverted hooves:
  When you
Turned and composed your last look at Raloo.

First leaf or last, you guessed
  Next year some tolerant branch would bend
To others' April or October thoughts,
  And the same stones submit,
  Still sentenced to parenthesis,
To the same wheels honed by identical ruts,
  While you,
Boxed in a frame, reflected on Raloo.

Now, decades after you turned
  Away from unanswering angels and
The easy virtue of the countryside,
  Your picture hangs on a wall
  With views of Carnlough and Glenarm,
Without a hint of how the colours bled
  When you
Cried out for affirmation at Raloo.

AN ATTIC IN HOLBORN

A window-plant grasps at crippled air
Reprieved from the rancid town; a chair
Condones the abdicated coat;
The candle's tongue-tied in cadaverous wax;
Torn manuscripts curl scattered round the box:
And, white as his face, the valedictory note
Is his receipt to fortune for his lot.

Below, life rustles in the waking town.
Light scales the curtains; windows yawn.
Thumped mats fawn welcome. Stubbornly,
A voice rehearses fragments of a tune.
A drayhorse kicks up saffron sparks from stone.
And gulls cut inland from the esturary,
Where tethered sails fret for the open sea.

GIG

Reaching to autograph fanatical hands,
You stand perhaps where I
Gormlessly missed the dolly-catch,
Young watchful wolves in a ring.
The hoods have spared the Methodist church hall.

My son, my brother also trod those boards,
Young croupier of applause,
Ace who outplayed the shuffling pack;
While I, dealt awkward hands,
Failed to conform, and never followed suit.

BARNARDO BOY

Trousers too loose, too long —
Toulouse, Toulon, in school vernacular —
Cuffing the kneecaps, head cropped to the bone;
Rough and recalcitrant
In class and yard, he was peripheral:
A kind of gipsy; Jew who'd married out.

Though he was tolerant
Of blackboard quip and badinage,
He kept a cutting edge on his resolve
Not to be cowed or conned
By circus discipline: the paper hoops,
Life tamed to tied or studied attitudes.

So no one's innocence
Was generous enough to tolerate
His declaration of uncertain love
When, surreptitiously,
Under the sloping counter of the desk,
He showed himself to shiny big-eyed girls.

HOT-CROSS BUNS

Flapping a flaccid hand —
(Imagine a handbell
Cuffing a cardboard street;
Add a castle cocked on a hill) —
She skirts the china dog
Matter-of-fact on the hearth,
The standard lamp, the what —
Not, and the paper shell
Of a fan in the summer grate:
While, miming her, the boy,
Watching his language, shapes
To shake his spurious bell,
His words to consonance;
Small fellow-traveller,
Agnostically aware
Of out-at-elbow streets
Incensed, incredulous,
The window sceptical:
Its outward gaze on bread-and-dripping lives.

LOVE

Now, after tea-time, when the spoilsport sun
Abandons lawns, good evening hesitates;
Say like a traveller bent on distances,
Anticipating night. Or like the man
Turned at the gate as if to memorise
The ivy's scribbled geography,
Each window's narrowing leaden-lidded eye.

Who reaches down accommodatingly
To take her hand and squire her dancing feet
Askew up to the corner, murmuring
Familial phrases, educating her
In names of trees, and verbalising sounds
Of home-birds hunkering down before
Night twitches closed the curtains, shades the light:

Good hand in daughter's hand, the hidden one
Conspiratorial in a pocket where
Pre-emptive murder threatens a by-blow;
His thoughts, observed for later, less concerned
With holed-up mistress quickening in distress
Than with the tart ambivalence
Of love turning a cheek for his goodnight.

BROTHERS-IN-LAW

Waiting for counsel in the hall,
You contemplate
A young man and a prison officer,
Attentive, affable,
Their heads together, shoulders intimate:
Then, unionists, separatists,
The handcuffs' wicked bangles on their wrists.

And say, within that context, they
Could equally
Be co-defendant, fellow-prisoner;
And both accomplices
Of that third party who goes home for tea
And passes time with friends,
After he's washed off judgment from his hands.

BALLAD SINGER: CHICHESTER STREET

1

Cheek by Law Courts' jowl,
The Variety Market stalls
For a further stay, and trades
Upon the Law's delays;
And, taking its own time,
Dallies, procrastinates,
But gets its business done
While the morning's fresh, and the sun's
Still rooflines short of the Sirocco Works,
And justices confer
Over a judgment, under their antique wigs.

2

She shrugs into her song
Of bright May mornings, lugs
The threadbare sentiments
Up off their knees to sing;
While, look, on the firemen's tower,
A young French officer
Steps from a picture book
And calls *To arms! To arms!*
Whereas, waxed water-clear,
The gallant engines stand,
Machines of mercy and
Manipulators of anarchic fire;
And shrewish women shop
Shrewdly around the stalls, closed to her song.

3

But: *here and there* you say
With wry inconsequence
To someone in your head,
Italicising words,
Continuing comrades of
Comfort from the war:
And here and there a petal. For —
As litigants congregate
Softfooted in the hall,
Whose marble walls reflect
Contorted images
Of miscast actors nervous of the play —
Miss Primrose, virginal
In wig and gown, cravat
Chucking her chin, evades, declines, deflects
Advancing glances, here
And there, a petal, glad-eyed, thought-caressed,
From mid-term dainty solemn dresden face.

4

You enter; feign to cringe
Before the petulant head.

She redlipreads, lips through the list.
(If you had waited, she'd have sung your song,
Shawled arms akimbo in the street).
Leafs through the list, wrist intimate with lace.
(Abandoned to, abandoned in her song).

THE ROUND POND

Later, you say, you will compare,
Not just with photographs,
Your recollection of
This place, already fiction in your mind,
But with those earlier memories of
Nostalgic stories told on evenings now
Themselves part of the dayligone,
The bittersweet
And legendary outback of the mind.

So, passive in the sunshine now,
You watch a steadying kite
Clean as a whistle shin
Up staggering altitudes, but note the man
Feeding the string, who, cat-eyed, covertly,
Is author and producer of the play,
A J. M. Barrie of the park,
Whose fantasy
Trails back at tea-time into his fussing hands.

WALLED GARDEN, IRISH STREET

That old walled garden, where
Among staid eighteenth-century trees
A cuckoo rang its flat ironic bell,
Seemed even then
Only a lull, a gracious interval
Missed, or dismissed by storm,
A pardoned pleasance where
Sun ivied on the wall
And breezes arched catfooted on the leaves.

What have you made from that
Windfall, or other intervals
Between recurring storms, while cuckoo-clocks,
Vox populi,
Proclaim false summers from constraining springs,
Other than keep ajar
Conclusions, premises,
Accommodatingly,
For whitefaced revelation at the door?

REMAINDERS

On Exhibition Road,
Given dry weather, you are sure to find
Remainders spread like bait
On tables by the door.
Old masters sprawl, reduced, in modern dress,
Abandonedly, to lure
The hurrying eye, the wet inquiring thumb.

Out for a paper, or
A matutinal stroll round Thurloe Square,
Sidetracked, compulsively
You'll probe for treasure trove
Lost in the lurid jungle, seeking out
With credulous fingertips —
As always — the remaindered Holy Grail.

Embarrassed by old friends
In dishabille, the masterpiece recast
As story-of-the-film,
The television-play,
Nevertheless you're liable to find
Among the cover-girls
Forgotten poets, banished novelists.

Then heart and hands extend
With undiminished gratitude and greed;
You even count the coins,
Make shelf-space in your mind.
But they are all at home: originals,
Pursued decades ago
Through long-demolished shops, and bought for love.

IN PASSING

At the piano singing,
In trained contralto, songs
By Schubert, or stiltedly playing
Demanding pieces from her repertoire,
Familial like photographs —

Hardly so much it seems
A passive memory,
A locked parenthesis,
As, what was the word, interpolation, a
Laying on of hands.

She plays from memory now,
And looks with a neutral gaze
From new-found distances;
An incarnation of light, absorbed, although
Comprising yesterdays.

SURVIVOR

In early summer snatched
Into whatever alien element
Or separate dream, she could
Given a voice declare
That all those unpermitted years,
Extended to others, have edged away like a dream,
Leaving only a pared phrase, a glance's glint
And flurried lipless cries
Sifted by weeds short of the open shore.

Tidying her hair,
One who survived declared
It was another world
It was as if
Some other had performed her part;
Or more as if
She'd found a letter written long ago
Purporting to be hers:
Or even more as if
She'd come upon a shiny photograph
Of once-upon-a-time, and cried
Alas for a slip of a girl with her winning smile.

WELSH FUNERAL: CARNMONEY

Only the daffodils,
Young hardy trumpeters,
Stood up to the sleet's despite, the wind's harangue,
    While, circumscribed by wreaths,
    Stiff in his Sunday best,
Tom Davies held his breath as the spades rang,
    Soil eructed on wood,
    And the preacher reasoned with God.

The argumentative hand
Knuckled on knee to cram
The briar's bowl or pluck to brandish a phrase,
    Conformed in a gesture of prayer;
    And, backed by daffodils,
His valley-verdant, dark-down-under voice
    Rolled from hills and dales
    Of the wind, homesick for Wales.

Muscling in music then,
Propping up pits of grief,
They hewed from light-and-dark ambivalence,
    Shouldering wind and rain,
    Their paeans and laments;
And, exile's face behind the citizen's,
    Myth-harried and myth-blessed,
    Hymns of the dispossessed.

Ambivalent citizen,
Reluctant patriot,
I thought of Ballinderry in the spring
When Samuel Ferguson
Mourned Thomas Davis, and
Quickened like leaves to his greenfinger song;
And said: Tom Davies will
Recruit the daffodil.

THE GARDEN OF REMEMBRANCE

Grown old in sinecure,
The cenotaph's alert
Only when brigadiers and clerics, hard
Hats and jowls, municipal collars, the
Militia of establishment,
Pout in parade to lay
On Victory Days
Their wreaths of poppycock.

Dismissed, the ghosts decamp,
Bugles and flags at rest,
And statues turn back to the City Hall,
Where in the twilight, through kiss-livid lips,
Lovers nostalgically recall,
Only to lay,
Ghosts of their disparate pasts.

THE GIRL

Was there a girl; or did
You conjure from thin air,
One August evening, walking above the shore —

Striking an attitude
Against rocks straddling the strand —
A figure hearkening from the hinterland,

Stirring and stirred by your blood,
To still life on a coast
Where spume spits back the losers and the lost?

Or: young, inhibited,
Did you retard your pace
Short of the candour of an actual face?

THE MILKMAN

Quick apparition on the step,
Your small change clattering in his fist,
He hugged effulgent in his other grip
A baby that he seemed to think you'd lost.

Proprietorial delight
In parenthood was tempered with
Grief for an unremembered loss. Her throat
Ovalled a word too fragile for the mouth.

GOING TO CHURCH ONE MORNING

Apprehensive of bells —
Like children tumbling to tell;
Clashbags at the gate;
Ringmasters, breezy interlocutors,
Pre-empting rehearsed events —

Securing your smile,
Infallible father support,
Walking backwards to school,
The girl in her new white dress, her face
        like a flower,
Wide-eyed, to a new roll-call;

While, beckoning down,
The saints in their windows trace,
With halo in hand,
Profiles of childhood peeping through masquerade,
Illuminating their vows.

51

HIGH LOW

When he is being pompous or afraid,
He hides behind his teaching-voice
And keeps his eye on what he's said,
Bidding his words beware. That I've observed.

But when a schoolmate, long since anglicised,
Called to astound him with his speech
And dapper culture subsidised
From rates and taxes, then the unreserved

Vernacular he'd spluttered as a child
Broke from his mouth, and rioted
Like dandelions in a field
Where trespass was an easement they'd preserved.

BIRTHDAY POEM

At fifty, I suppose, you'll count the change,
Number your debtors and your creditors,
Adjust accounts, write off old loves, and put
The reckoning in your diary. But, or yet,

You'll also scatter starling glances over
A set shrugged shoulder soldiering through time
Back to a time when, with so much unsaid,
Life was a girl always a step ahead.

THE HOLE

Precociously out of his mind
With politics and sex and poetry,
He was obliged to stand

With hucksters assailing the Hole,
Jostling to catch the bales of trussed-up words,
The early-morning kill.

Young swain of literature,
He postured for his clap of thunder from
The mews's aperture.

If I had my rights, Yeats cried,
I'd be the Duke of Ormonde. Covertly,
Campaigners in *his* head

Hoisted him in above,
A young blade cutting loose among the straw,
Brandishing words like love.

A WORD IN HIS EAR

I gave him my word.
Intimations I said,
Releasing it to infiltrate
Beyond his public attitudes
Into a personal sanctum where — instead
Of late conferments: gown, certificate,
The pensioner's clock, municipal platitudes —
He cries out to an absent editor
For a last proof.

REUNION

Within a fractured province; less:
Inside a town obscene with barricades
And rifles at the ready, bless,
God or Anon, before the picture fades

A congregation of four friends
Gathered to acclaim in separate ways
A long-loved book's rebirth, old hands
Renewing friendship with a wry surprise.

Before they fracture bread or spill
Wine's secret into glass, let glass reflect
Four faces singly stemmed, until
They share the wine's slow statement, and extract

From dregs and crumbs a sacrament
For two believing, two agnostic minds,
Each singular ingredient
Familial under the author's hosting hands:

As, after thirty years, the voice
Of that small masterpiece binds them together,
A four-leafed clover, to rejoice
That common ground survives inclement weather

THE TRAVELLER

Coming at evening —
Midsummer, with the mowers murmuring,
Handclap of shears;
Autumn's curtailment, when the gas
Mantles hirstle and cry at the shortening days;
And Christmas-time —:

After the blandishments,
The ritual exchanges, he remains,
A surrogate
Postman important with the news,
To nibble gossip like wine-biscuits, sip
At peccancies.

Socks uniformly rolled
Like gallant puttees round abandoned shins,
His bicycle
At ease against a window-sill,
He licks his pencil while you distantly
Call from the shelves.

Gleaming with medal-brass,
Its fetlocks feathered, the huge blinkered horse
Next midday heaves
The hooded cart from door to door.
Oats, dribbled from the feedbag, countrify
The dayligone.

THE ASTORIA

Outlandish frontager,
Confronting thoroughfare
With unabashed bucolic innocence,
Its old glass signalling
Back to the sparking trams;
Decades of privet, cemetery paths,
A tepid greenhouse, couped red wheelbarrows:

Shorn from the hinterland,
It mimed suburban ways;
Rubbed shoulders with the shops and houses, paid
Its taxes, and observed
The early-closing day;
But stoically, if absentmindedly,
It kept its *thereness* like a stranded tree.

Abruptly it was gone.
You noticed first the lack
Of glass, then took in all the emptiness
Where bushes along the paths
Had made a natural maze.
Laid out along the slope the apple-trees
Were statues in a morgue, dead, falsified.

Hoarding and scaffolding
Thwarted a sneak preview.
But nobody was moved to entertain
A plea for pleasance when
That local Eden changed
Into a hothouse for exotic love,
Lettuce supplanted by a let's-pretend.

Sixpenny patrons, we
Embraced in the back-stalls
Sophistication and unnatural warmth;
Inhaled America
And Ealing's England, but
Translated them to Ballyhackamore,
Ecumenists in the vernacular.

Now *it's* succinctly gone,
The skyline engineered
To prop a concrete coffin. In your mind,
Circle and stalls line up
To join old greenery
Vegetating in the hinterland,
Where yesterday perhaps is still today.